WIN THE
INTERVIEW,
LAND THE OFFER

RANEISHA B. LOVE

About the Author

Meet Raneisha! She is the owner of Prestigious Resume & Writing Source, a stellar resume writing & career services firm. Raneisha specializes in producing expertly crafted & creatively designed resumes. She is also a career coach and adviser.

Although Louisiana based, she has clients in various states.

Raneisha focuses on personal branding and creating the best marketing tools for her clients. Resumes, cover letters, and interviewing are all marketing tools. Successful marketing is required to secure a career opportunity. With her career expertise, she has created a proven success guide to help job-seekers throughout their interviewing processing.

@THEWORLDCLASSWRITER

Purpose

This book was created to help job seekers to get hired. This success guide will focus on interview actions and key behaviours that recruiters are looking for. Knowing what recruiters are seeking and implementing these strategies in the guide will greatly increase your interview success rate.

There are many candidates that are a great fit for positions they apply for, however interviewing may not be a strong point for them. This often leads to not getting the offer. This success guide was created to help ease the process of interviewing. Our ultimate goal is for you to feel empowered after reading and land the career of your dreams!

www.iwritemagic.com

Contents

CHAPTER 1: Receiving The Invitation

There can be so many mixed emotions when preparing for an interview. You may feel excited, nervous, or even fearful. You may feel excited about new career opportunities.

You may be nervous about the interview process. You may be fearful about not being able to sell yourself, impress the recruiter, and land the job. All of these are natural feelings and reactions. However, this guide was created to help you overcome all odds and easily land that job offer.

CHAPTER 2: Know Their Name(s)

Learn the name of the person/people that will interview you. Prior to your interview, inquire about what type of interview you will have. Will you interview with just one person or will you interview with a panel? The best time to ask would be while you're receiving your initial invitation to interview. However, if you did not gather these details prior you can always call or email for verification.

For example, if you are interviewing with two people you should bring two copies of your resume for each of them. You then want to pull out your manila folder (inside your briefcase) and hand a copy to each person.

Knowing the number of interviewers will help you prepare. Be sure to bring extra copies, just in case. It is always better to have more than needed versus less than needed.

Obtain the first and last name of the person/people interviewing you. If your interviewer's name is Jefferey Smith.

Upon meeting him, address him as Mr. Smith. For example, "Hello Mr. Smith, what a pleasure to meet you." You'd want to say something similar while extending your hand for a firm (meaningful) handshake.

CHAPTER 3: Don't Show Up Empty-Handed

It's not a good idea to show up to an interview empty-handed. It demonstrates lack of preparation. See both examples below.

Erica is well qualified for the position. She shows up for the interview empty-handed.

Erin is well qualified for the position. She shows up for the interview with her portfolio containing multiple copies of her resume, cover letters, references, certifications, and awards.

Remember most people won't show up with these items. Most people only show up with themselves.

By bringing your portfolio, this is a great way to make yourself stand out from the rest of the candidates.

Although both candidates are qualified, who would you be more impressed by? Erin, right. Erin went the extra mile and demonstrated preparation.

Preparation is key! How can you go the extra mile?

Some may not have certifications or awards to bring, which is perfectly fine. You can create a list of your achievements, a list of your skills, or even letters of recommendation.

CHAPTER 4: Memorize Your Resume

Familiarizing yourself with your resume is another great way to stand out.

It is extremely important to MEMORIZE your resume.

Recruiters want to discuss what you present them, therefore they will want to discuss your resume. You are not fully prepared, if you can't discuss it without looking at it.

Remember, preparation is key. Most candidates fix it and forget it.

Once their resume has landed them an interview, they never refer to it again. Then at the time of the interview, the recruiter may bring up something that they can't answer right away.

CHAPTER 5: Compliment Your Recruiter

We all love compliments.

Be personable! Develop a connection with the recruiter. Remember, people hire people they like. Find a way to bond before the interviewing process begins.

Compliment your recruiter. Don't say things such as "You look nice or you smell good." That is very broad and unimpressive.

A great example would be "You're wearing teal today, that's my favorite color!" You would say this with a big smile! This comment/compliment would open the door to friendly conversation. You want to find something in common with them. It doesn't matter if your true favorite color is purple.

CHAPTER 6: First Impressions Matter

You can only make a first impression once, so make sure your first impression is impeccable.

Arrive at least an hour and 15 minutes earlier than scheduled.

You can wait in your car and review your notes that you should have prepared prior to your interview.

These notes can be your career highlights or anything that makes you best suited for the role.

Do you know specifically where you are going? In some cases, we apply at places we have never physically been before which makes us rely on GPS to get there. What happens if you are going to an unfamiliar place and your means of GPS fails?

What happens if you are in route and there are traffic delays? You always want to plan for delays and give yourself extra time. You don't want your first impression explaining why you couldn't make it on time.

CHAPTER 7: Dress The Part

Remember, you're not fully dressed without your smile. Your smile can symbolize openness, warmth, and friendliness. Your smile is also inviting so don't forget to wear it. Don't forget to display great body language. Great eye contact is also important.

Your appearance needs to scream professionalism. If your appearance is not professional, no matter what you say or do it's a strong chance your recruiter will not take you seriously. This diminishes your chance of receiving the offer.

CHAPTER 8: What Benefits Can You Offer The Company?

Prior to your interview, know what benefits you are bringing to the company. Consider these 3 questions

- Will you make money for the company?
- Will you save money for the company?
- What unique problem will you solve?

How will you contribute? Be clear and compelling of the value you can bring to them.

Chapter 9 Stay Positive

Never insult any of your previous employers during an interview! Don't say anything negative. Even if you have legit reasons to be angry about your previous employers/bosses/co-workers... don't express that during this time.

Don't dwell on unfortunate situations on your last job, instead focus on what lies ahead. Once offered the position, it'll be new people, new beginnings, new challenges, and new opportunities.

CHAPTER 10: Appearance, Hygiene

Your apparel should never be oversized or undersized. Your apparel should never be too revealing. Your apparel should never be too long or too short. Your apparel should never be distracting. Stay away from loud colors and distracting patterns.

Don't go overboard on perfume or cologne. Don't go overboard on jewelry and accessories. You don't want to be flashy. Remember to avoid distracting or unprofessional hairstyles. For example, you don't want to interview with a mohawk.

Professionally tailored suits, ties, slacks, collared shirts, pocket squares, knee length dresses, knee length skirts, dress socks, and dress shoes are highly recommended items.

Apparel must be clean, crisp, neat, and pressed. Solid neutral colors are always preferred.

CHAPTER 11: High Heels

Let's face it, all women are unique and have different styles. Some of us love high heels and can't go a day without them.

Some of us wear them only on special occasions. Some of us find them uncomfortable. Some of us wear them dependent upon our outfits. Some of us don't wear them at all.

Ladies if you are comfortable in heels, wear them. Our company always recommend staying four inches or below. Also, a solid neutral color is preferred. If heels are not your comfort zone you do not have to wear them.

You do not want to walk wobbly, appear unbalanced, or even uncomfortable during your interview. If you elect to wear heels, wear a pair that you can comfortably walk in.

CHAPTER 12: Tip for Ladies

Add a brooch to your attire. You want to pick one small to medium in size. Preferably a solid gold or silver one. Brooches are very sophisticated and can make you stand out.

Brooches can symbolize strength and confidence. Remember you want to stand out from other candidates, most will not wear one.

CHAPTER 13: Tip to easily stand out

Prepare a one page professional biography and give it to your recruiter at the time of your interview. Most of your competition will not do this and by having a professional bio you can easily impressive your recruiter.

A professional biography/bio is a narrative summary of your life and work. It often highlights one's achievements-like in a resume-but may also feature one's vision, mission, defining values, interests, and hobbies.

A biography can tell the why of someone's work-not just the what-and is a representation of your career history, showcasing your most critical career accomplishments. It is often a one- page narrative, although length may vary depending on the purpose.

CHAPTER 14: What Do You Know About The Company?

If your recruiter asked you this question today, how would you respond? How convincing would your response be? Would your response outshine the response of your competitors?

Would there be a long pause for you to think of an answer? Long pauses and delayed responses are frowned upon.

CHAPTER 15: What Should
You Know About The Company?

Write this information down so you can refer to it and increase your chances of remembering it.

Days or even weeks prior to your interview research the company and obtain their background. You'll want to research the following questions.

- Who are the leaders of the company?
- What is the company's mission? How long have they been around?
- How does this company benefit its consumers and employees? What are some challenges they face?
- Who are their competitors? How can you contribute and be an asset to the team?

CHAPTER 16: What Are
Your Skills and Qualifications?

Days or even weeks prior to your interview write down your unique skills, qualifications, and your accomplishments. Once you have written this information down, compare it to the skills and qualifications listed under the career description posted. Make a short list of bullet points that are easy to remember.

The purpose of this is to provide talking points during your interview. If there are certain achievements that you would like to highlight during your interview the short list of bullet points will help you.

CHAPTER 17: Unexperienced

If you are a new graduate with little to no experience, you can always talk about the skills you've obtained while pursing your degree. Ensure that these skills match with the skills needed for the job that you've applied for. If you are switching careers, you can use this strategy as well.

For example, if you have been in retail for years and you want a new career in healthcare. What skills have you obtained in retail that you can also use in healthcare? These skills are considered transferable skills. Write these skills down and discuss them during your interview.

CHAPTER 18: Tips to Avoid Nervousness

Always show confidence!

Remember you never want to appear arrogant or cocky, instead you want to be confident in your abilities. By using the techniques referenced above it will help avoid nervousness and increase your preparation. Be ready to explain your transferable skills.

What skills have you obtained in your previous history that you can bring to the new role? Write these transferable skills down and review it regularly. Be prepared to answer behavioural based interview questions as well. Increasing your preparation will decrease your nervousness.

CHAPTER 19: Practice, Practice, Practice,

Research most commonly asked interview questions. Prepare the most suited and professional response for these questions.

Practice saying your responses aloud. You want to hear your own responses so you can look for opportunities of improvement. If you can have a family member or friend they can practice with you.

Remember for the actual interview you don't want to sound rehearsed, you want your responses to sound natural/professional. Don't just wing it. Don't just show up unprepared and see how things go. The more you practice the better the outcome. Take time and properly plan and prepare.

CHAPTER 20: Career Levels

When applying for careers, read both the position description and career level very carefully. For example, a software engineer 2 at one organization can be considered a software engineer 1 or 3 at another organization.

CHAPTER 21: Salary Research

Research the average salary for the career that you are seeking. There are tools to give you a better idea as to what employers are paying for the career you are pursing.

Glassdoor.com and Salary.com are just a couple among many available to you online. Always familiarize yourself with the current market rate for your target position.

CHAPTER 22: Never Bring Up Compensation, First

Always remember to let the recruiter bring up compensation first. If the recruiter would like to move forward in the hiring process, they will bring up this discussion on their own timing.

CHAPTER 23: Salary Negotiation

It is very important to have a realistic expectation of the appropriate salary for the role, always consider geographic location, skills, and responsibility level. If you are asked to give a number, provide a salary range based on the research you have done.

If you receive an offer that is less than expected, explain the value that you bring. Show details as to why your value should be higher. Never ask for more money, without being able to explain your worth.

CHAPTER 24: Never Ask, "How well it went?"

Once your interview is complete, never ask the recruiter
"How did I do?" This not only puts the recruiter in an awkward position,
but shows that you are unsure of yourself, and have low self-awareness. Aim to be so confident in yourself and your skills that you
don't need reassurance!

CHPATER 25: Don't Disclose Too Much

Never talk about what the job can do for you personally

For example, don't discuss how you would benefit from the pay increase or business hours.

Don't discuss how you would be closer to home or how you prefer the commute. Never discuss anything that shows how you would benefit personally.

CHAPTER 26: Corporate Risk!

Hiring is a gamble.

Hiring you is a corporate risk! Taking on a new job can be a major life event for both you and your family. Various factors must be considered. Things such as your commute, your compensation, your benefits, your responsibilities, your new team, your direct reports, and so much more.

Be mindful that as you are busy considering this new opportunity & its potential advantages/ disadvantages and how it will impact both you and your family, the hiring authority is doing the same with you.

CHAPTER 27: Remember It's About Them, Not You

Don't make the interview about you, make it about them.

Focus on what benefits you bring to the company and be able to explain these things to the recruiter.

CHAPTER 28: Signs They Are Not Interested In You

This is just an FYI or helpful hint. One major sign that shows a recruiter's lack of interest is them asking you very few questions. Three of less questions would not be adequate.

If the recruiter is not asking enough questions to learn about you and determine if you are a great fit for the company that can be a giveaway that they are not interested. The more questions they ask, the better! The fewer questions they ask, more likely they have already decided that you won't receive the offer.

CHAPTER 29: Never Show Desperation

We understand, life happens. At times, some of us can be at a stage in our lives where we are unemployed and need a source of income immediately. However, under no circumstances should you show signs of desperation during your interview.

Never say things like "I'll do anything", "I'll do whatever it takes", or "I really need this job." You don't want to show any signs of needing sympathy or pity. Care about getting the job, be focused, and determined without appearing desperate.

CHAPTER 30: Counter Questions

Never answer a question with a question. For example, if the recruiter asks, "Tell me about yourself." Your response should not be "What would you like to know?" Never counter a question. It is unprofessional and demonstrates lack of preparation. Always provide a direct answer.

CHAPTER 31: Short Responses

You don't want to have one-word answers or have extremely short responses. Additionally, you want to keep in mind you don't want to have long draining responses neither. Keep your responses conversational.

CHAPTER 32: Ask Questions

Always ask questions after your interview, even if your recruiter covered everything. Not asking questions demonstrates both lack of interest and preparation.

We recommend our clients to bring a list of questions to ask at the end of the interview. This is prepared beforehand. If you don't, you will most likely forget what questions you have. Remember it is best to ask between 3-5 questions concluding your interview.

CHAPTER 33: What's Next...

At the end of your interview always find out what's next. You can simply ask when a hiring decision will be made. This way, you're not in the dark and you know what to expect. Most recruiters will share their expected timeframe for deciding.

CHAPTER 34: Follow Up

Follow up strategies are important. Don't forget to thank the recruiter within 24-48 hours after your interview. You can thank them via email or phone. When you make contact, it is important to touch on the following 5 topics.

Express gratitude and appreciation for their time/ consideration.

Demonstrate your attentiveness, by mentioning something specific you both discussed. This shows your email/call is not generic.

Show you're interested in the position by expressing excitement about the opportunity.

Welcome them to contact you, should any questions arise.

Express self-confidence. Tell them how you can not only meet their expectations but exceed them.

CHAPTER 35: Encouragement

Whether your next interview is for a meaningless job just to pay the bills or a satisfying career, remember to always give it your absolute best. If you have not found career satisfaction yet, establish an action plan to obtain it.

Never give up on your goals and aspirations! You can achieve anything through hard work and dedication. This concludes our success guide. Hopefully, you have gathered many takeaways and feel fully equipped for your next interview.

PROVEN STRATEGIES
FOR INTERVIEW SUCCESS!

Made in the USA
Middletown, DE
17 December 2019